VERSES FOR THE 21ST CENTURY

ADAM AND EVE ON THE INTERNET

Alfred W. Israelstam

Cover Illustration by Beatrice Ruden Israelstam

 CHICAGO SPECTRUM PRESS
1571 SHERMAN AVENUE
EVANSTON, IL 60201
1-800-594-5190

Printed in Canada.

Library of Congress Card Catalog Number: 97-65211

10 9 8 7 6 5 4 3 2 1

ISBN: 1-886094-61-6

DEDICATION

The rhythmic cadence of my beating heart
Replete with resonance required in rhyme
Though meaning may not surface every time
Endowed these sonnets from the very start

But essays in this disparate collection
Would not have seen the light of day in print
Unless my daughter Frances had my dint
Of dedication culled them with affection

Assembled, edited for publication
As only loving daughters ever do
Selecting paper, type, and book design
Entitled as she is to acclamation
If you do not enjoy them when you're through
Responsibility is only mine.

L'Envoi

Kudos though belongs to yet another
My gifted artist wife—Francie's mother.

TABLE OF CONTENTS

ON WORDS

AUTOBIOGRAPHY

ON POETRY

HISTORY

ACCEPTANCE

COMMENTARY

VIEWPOINTS

RELIGION

SCIENCE AND TECHNOLOGY

THANKS

INTRODUCTION

Verses for the 21st Century: Adam and Eve on the Internet is a book of love and promise. My father is a poet who is always writing poetry. It's as simple as that. For as long as I can remember, he captured and synthesized his world in words written on pieces of paper or in small notebooks. Carefully chosen words tethered his experiences to papers which he routinely tucked into his pockets, his briefcase, and then into overflowing drawers. Sometime later he would unpack these notes, contemplate their value, and poems would emerge. He worked at these verses. He studied the works of others. He experimented with other styles, but time and again he returned to the structure, discipline, and form of the sonnet.

As a child I was awed by the breadth of his vocabulary and the rhythm of his words. I drew strength and pleasure from his persistent search for words and derivations in dictionaries. I cheered when for his eighty-seventh birthday he bought himself a new set of Encyclopaedia Britannica, because there was so much he still wanted to learn.

My mother is an artist who creates beautiful works of art and beautiful home environments for us to live within. It's as simple as that. In her search for new ideas and media, she began to explore computer graphics. The cover and chapter graphics of this book are her creations.

As the child of an attorney-poet and an artist-designer I see this volume as a book of their love and commitment—to each other, to life, and to tomorrow. I see this book as a book of promise—to take these words, ideas and images into the 21st century to be savored and contemplated.

- Frances Israelstam Levin

ACKNOWLEDGMENTS

My gratitude to my family is boundless.

I acknowledge my debt to each member: from my parents, siblings, wife, son and daughter, nieces and nephews, through to my grandchildren and great grandchildren.

All have participated in the pages of this book.

I hope you will enjoy meeting them. They are your neighbors, and growing closer each day via the Internet.

Special thanks to Dorothy Kavka for editing the manuscript and to my daughter Frances and her husband David for many hours spent proofreading the text, designing the layout, and encouraging this humble poet.

FOREWORD

The sonnets contained in this book reflect most of my prejudices, convictions, and beliefs. I count it no small privilege, when the history of man's governments over his fellow-man is reviewed, to have found freedom from the many strictures that bind us by our politics, religion, economics, science, and art—to say what I please without fear or favor. If the stanzas provide a single person who survives me with hope, I shall not have been here and gone for nothing. That hope, however vain or fruitful, lent meaning to my existence.

I love America, where I was born early in the 20th century. My religion offers me solace and discipline. My modest economic circumstances afford me sufficient leisure. Science advances my culture, and art ennobles and enables me to express myself. Within that firm framework, I find resilience and stress, a tension between me and my society, between conformance and rebellion. Society, with four million people living nearby me and six billion people on the planet Earth, is overwhelming. My imagination compels it to stand still, a tentatively stalled frame in an endlessly moving picture.

These sonnets were written in anticipation of the upcoming 21st century. Rhythms and rhymes, however trivial, are part of our literary inheritance. Children respond to them, but a fondness seems to persist, even among those of my vintage, for recollections to contemplate. Our poets are inheritors of the prophets of old. They summon us and challenge us to be aware of ourselves, to think noble thoughts, to dream of perfecting ourselves because we know our failings.

As I address the small planet on which I was born, comfortable in the awareness it will hold my remains when it no longer needs me, I am confronted by an oxymoron: I am at once filled with both trepidation and relief: no one knows more about God than I, and no one knows less.

This book of sonnets addresses a responsive character—that character is you. You, the reader, are invited to enter into a conversation, to agree or disagree in an effort to blend life with art since reason is a mental sensation and logic is a social convention. You decide if you can utilize what I experienced. These essays are like crumbs to feed the birds among you who, nibbling on them, may fly a little higher as you survey this wonderful planet spread out below you.

- AWI, October, 1996

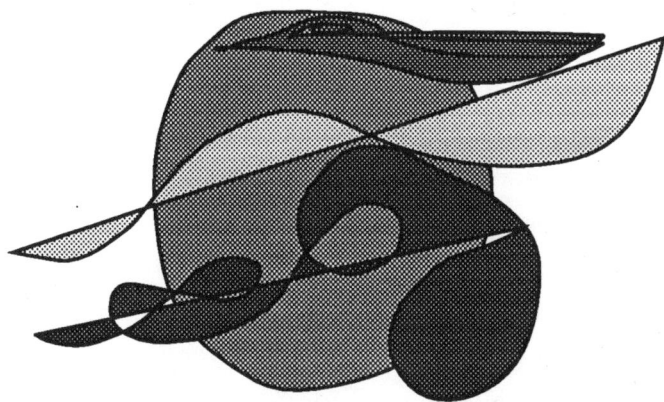

ON WORDS

AWAY WITH ANGST

If you are eager for an explanation
Why thought, idea, image come to mind
Arising randomly, or else designed
Consider your unspoken expectation

Which arches from indifference to elation
Depending on the way you've been inclined
Unless like others you are flying blind
Between despondency and exultation

Your world grows large, or shrinks into a fraction
As problems you create claim your attention
Or nag at you—as you seek some way out
Unless your conscience screams at you for action
Which, followed through, erases apprehension
You should relax—time will erase your doubt.

L'Envoi

If from your whirling gears you disengage
You may find respite when you turn the page.

LAVISH LEGACY

My friend who said to me, "some die, you'll perish"
Knew well my fondness for a word or phrase
Words such as "like" rejected; I might "cherish"
Delight in speech would linger all my days

Fond phrases now were lost to winds and flames
My verses vanished, disappeared, dissolved
Too late, my friends for prattle, fun, and games
My pleasures, like my pains, have been resolved

Instead, I leave you with a simple thought
A single word that I was conscious of
The residue of all that I was taught
To family and friends, you have my love
A word is like an orange, remove the peel
Then taste—it helps remember how to feel.

L'Envoi

Words can be lambent, floating light and airy
They're waiting for you in the dictionary.

A WORLD OF WORDS

A word can lighten spirits on confession
Or burden you with stress upon the heart
Can sadden you when intimates depart
Or signify great joy by your expression

Distinguish common language from profession
Explain the image placed upon a chart
In all technology—can stop or start
Arouse a listless group when it's in session

Words indicate when music's fast or slow
Can march in serried ranks or single file
Their rhythm can be smooth or else exciting
Can signify your happiness or woe
Cause you to weep, or change into a smile
Declare a peace—or start the whole world fighting.

L'Envoi

A word may whisper, mumble, or it cries
Sometimes a word unuttered may be wise.

COMMUNICATING

Although we can't begin to understand
Words thought and used by all who've lived and died
Who dwelt in countries stretching far and wide
Wherever mankind trod upon the land

A patriarch who issued his command
Or sailor who left port on rising tide
Shrewd husband uttered to his cozened bride
In tribal village or in castle grand

Strange languages of those we never heard
Odd sounding voices foreign to our ear
Like blessings, some intoned before a meal
However sweet, insistent, or absurd
Though mumbled—or pronounced in accents clear
Words make assumptions of what people feel.

L'Envoi

While intellects go in and out of fashion
We do not err with words that show compassion.

JAWS OF PREJUDICE

How shall we know when untoward thoughts accrue
About the nature of the world and man
Though prejudice has thrived since time began
Demeaning others still is always new

Defaming is a crocodile's grip
An unrelenting clutch on some belief
That crushes someone else's life to grief
But illustrates imperfect scholarship

Try first compassion as the words escape
Whether or not the phrase is merited
Each word invented for a time and place
Proceed with caution rather than to ape
Those mindless words we have inherited
It makes less need for later saving face.

L'Envoi

Before an epithet bursts from your lung
You'll cause less grief if you will bite your tongue.

NOW HEAR THIS

A word is like a hammer that can strike
A blow to some idea you hold dear
Can crush your feelings, aggravate your fear
Or plug a hole sprung in your mental dike

A word can cut through feelings like a saw
To sever "truth" you earlier assumed
Slit error from a concept you presumed
Or smooth a surface rendered rough and raw

Like hammer, saw—a word can also drill
Bite deeply through a former satisfaction
Contentment turned and twisted in distraction
To leave a hole for misery to fill
Though words may badly damage how you feel
They likewise may soothe pain—to thereby heal.

L'Envoi

Since dreadful is the power in those tools
Beware of words from miscreants and fools.

A WORD TO THE WISE

Words misconstrued can obfuscate the sun
But clarified, they brighten life again
Explained, lend strength, become so helpful when
Those dark uncertainties may trouble one

Defined, they dress a thought in current fashion
Replace with gems a string of tawdry beads
Inspire others to heroic deeds
Reveal a thitherto concealed passion

May burnish what was previously duller
Depending on their presence in a form
Can hasten or delay the passing hour
Will sparkle with a blaze of glowing color
Used indiscriminately, cause a storm
Flash, then explode behind their power.

L'Envoi

Words can insinuate, thereby impair
Used heedlessly are hazardous—beware.

LEXICOLOGY

From birth, until I'm carried in a casket
I use my words to think, speak, read, and write
An effortless collection—it's as slight
As berries picked and carried in a basket

Those words gave me the names of things to eat
To calculate the minute or the hour
From root to stem, they blossom like a flower
A simple or an orthographic feat

For pleasure—or in order to be hired
A quarter-million words at beck and call
Are luxury—or labor—impulse varies
I value them as wealth to be acquired
How easy after that to find them all
Like precious gems concealed in dictionaries.

L'Envoi

Words planted prudently and cultivated
Yield rich rewards when they're premeditated.

PREJUDGMENT

An uttered prejudice, like cough or sneeze
Unguarded at the moment it arose
May harm us thoughtlessly the way it goes
Because its carelessness can spread disease

When feelings are transmuted into logic
There, reason quickly dons emotion's cloak
Can harm a person or entire folk
Whose hopes become depressed, hence biologic

Words come so easily to dress a thought
Which voices what's presumably believed
Belief accepting other's thoughts as magic
Religious/racial notions thus are bought
Resulting in the innocent aggrieved
Which all-too-often ends in something tragic.

L'Envoi

To falsely denigrate our equal status
Can lead another mindlessly to hate us.

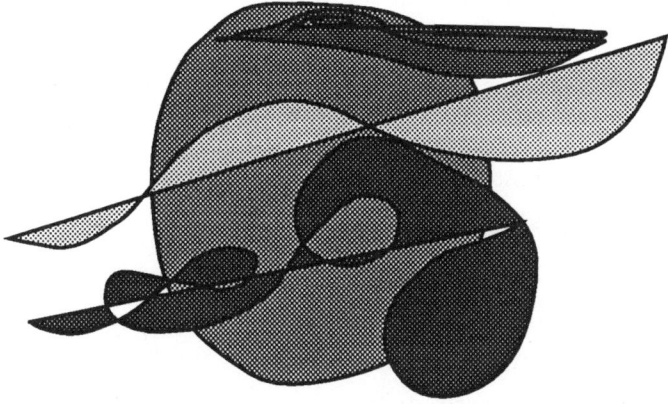

AUTOBIOGRAPHY

REVELATION

Astonishing what my belief can do
Assume reality in anything
God's Ten Commandments—fiber optics sing
Miraculous phenomena seem true

A flash across a synapse comes in view
Adjacent axons triggered, pop and ping
Awareness strikes—belief begins to bring
A latent mood upon me, old yet new

Strange feeling lying dormant in my heart
Or maybe soul, but something deep inside
Like biosocial, myth, or fairy elf
Implodes some covert craft or skill or art
Incredibly, as my eyes opened wide
I found I was believing in—myself.

L'Envoi

Belief was mine to choose—wherefore I chose
As doubt dissolved, self-confidence arose.

WHO AM I?

From infancy, what have I now become
So many persons—seen through others' eyes
My attitudes, and attributes, in sum
If told to me might jolt me with surprise

What culture I inherited informed me
To act with modesty—propriety
My family's ideals early warmed me
Toward ways to help improve society

But legacies produce peculiar traits
American—old European—Asian
I'm generous at times, but not in straits
Behavior depending on occasion
My slim attainments tell you I'm not very
Unusual—in fact—quite ordinary.

L'Envoi

Although to some I may add up to zero
I much prefer to think myself—a hero.

VAST DIFFERENCE

When I was young my father soon instilled
Ideas in my mind—or was it brain
My childish head was very early filled
With notions of the sacred and profane

I knew it made a difference if I lied
Though mostly I was honest as a youth
And I can safely say I always tried
To tell it like it was—to tell the "truth"

I still endeavor to remain the same
To tell the truth—the way it seems to me
Refrain from actions causing shame or blame
Yet there's a difference—maybe of degree
But with the passing years new views evolved
Too much of what was sacred had dissolved.

L'Envoi

Technology replaced that which I saw
Diminished what had earlier been awe.

ORNAMENTS

Like beads strung randomly around my neck
Not imitations—cheap—as so much waste
Or ordinary glass hung there in haste
Impetuously bought with cash or check

Nor manufactured by machines—hi-tech
Or artificial substance made with paste
But gleaming globes of most exquisite taste
That bear no sign of scratch, or mar, or fleck

These pearls are placed at different times—apart
Or close together—shining in their splendor
Held on a chain of gold, this ornament
Each pearl betokening what touched my heart
Beyond the price of gems from any vendor
Each celebrating a unique event.

L'Envoi

However beautiful and much desired
I add a pearl—only when inspired.

GROWING OLD

The "make believe" played with a childhood friend
Four score and more—those dream-like years before
Those days that now seem gone forevermore
A foolish game we both called "Let's Pretend"

But now approaching time I can't extend
Those fun-filled days marked by esprit de corps
The times I know full-well can be no more
Infirmities we can no longer mend

Yet there comes back to me the game we played
Although we knew pretensions were not so
Resigned these days that every life must end
This well-worn body currently decayed
However short the time before I go
I wander forth—still playing—Let's Pretend.

L'Envoi

Although we change the masks, and change the scene
We cherish most of all where we have been.

PLAYTHINGS

Those shiny objects of my aspiration
Which sparkled with a gleam of promised joy
Converted what was otherwise a toy
Into a moment of exhilaration

Envisioning fulfillment with delight
Remembering the joyous mood I'd feel
This play at life, approached with heady zeal
Excitement obfuscating clearer sight

As hope expanded into expectation
Imagination brightening my view
Spun rainbow bridges arched to cross in lieu
Of facts—until each ended—in frustration
But toys I loved—replaced in my affections
Still linger on in timeless recollections.

L'Envoi

Recalling toys of youth has made me pensive
But toys I want today are too expensive.

MY MEMORIES

So seldom now, my mind fills to the brim
Recalling scenes from my old neighborhood
Where I was young—and all the world seemed good
But time has cataracts—those scenes grown dim

Rash days of vigor—I was slim, and trim
Competed in all sports the best I could
I sang and danced as every person should
Reality arrived—my life grew grim

Imperative—each daily race now run
As duty toes me closely to the line
To keep my obligations up to date
I don't complain about the lack of fun
If you should ask, I'd say "I'm feeling fine"
But those old memories are scant of late.

L'Envoi

Those were the days—no drugs, no AIDS—no rock
Yet if I could I'd not turn back the clock.

TRANSGRESSION

When young, I often glowed with noble feeling
A bud before the flowering of youth
No answer was permissible but "truth"
I looked disdainfully at double-dealing

God sat enthroned above the highest ceiling
Who kept a wary eye were I uncouth
In playground, stadium, or private booth
When walking, running, on my bike when wheeling

No grey-edged doubt—but black and white were stark
A peccadillo would not be accepted
No cloud could block His penetrating sight
A sin would leave me tainted with a mark
No one could rescue me were I rejected
I had no choice—except to do what's "right."

L'Envoi

A word like "virtue" may be wearing thin
But has not yet grown obsolete—like "sin."

PERSONAL TESTAMENT

My father, rest in peace, created me
He nourished both my body and my mind
Taught me to search our Bible, helped me find
Such faith as leads me through life's mystery

Whence came undaunted strength which boldly tackles
Those worthy goals that challenge to compete
With eager eyes and ears, strong hands and feet
But sits on Holy Days, in tabernacles

Strange mystery—dear father gone—yet seems
To be alive—because I see your face
I hear your voice—remember your affection
They come to me as clearly as in dreams
It reassures: I, too, might leave a trace
To linger in somebody's recollection.

L'Envoi

Thereby live on—though lacking in sensation
Survive through kin's and friends' imagination.

FAIRY TALE FROG

Your sweet and tender patience waiting for
This frog to be transformed into a prince
Was starry-eyed—but often made me wince
Expecting me to change my nature, or

Transmute my voice—begin a lilting song
To modify my cacophonic croak
Though sounds you heard were words I never spoke
Since I knew better as we went along

Through all the years since first we found each other
You've lived like you believed your fairy tale
Convinced your expectations would not fail
You as my bride—and later as a mother
I watch you turning, restless in your sleep
Still dreaming that some day I'll make the leap.

L'Envoi

A frog who would a-wooing go, was wed
And found a lovely princess in his bed.

HUMILITY

I tried to be an intellectual
Impress my hearers I was highfalutin'
Dropped famous names in ways effectual
Like Ptolemy, Copernicus and Newton

I'd sound Aristotelian—Socratic
Whereby I'd overwhelm some simple soul
I'd dominate him, sounding so dogmatic
Persuade him I was firmly in control

But when I met a man who was perceptive
Intelligent—soft-spoken—words were few
Who saw the "other" side before he blamed
I recognized that he was more effective
Paid close attention til the man was through
Then swallowed hard, because I felt ashamed.

L'Envoi

It overcame me—I was deeply moved
I hope you find my manners have improved.

SITTING UP IN BED

A microchip slid out—I could not scan it
It slipped away til it was out of sight
Escaped from my computer into night
A floating fragment—but I did not plan it

That chip was I—with memories inscribed
Which diverse circumstances had created
With data I had earlier conflated
Whose meanings though had not yet been transcribed

Then came the dawn—the chip was back in place
To scribe again the crowded day's events
Where life meets death—as quickly as a wink
Adrift that moment I was out in space
With small concern for dollars or for cents
It gave me opportunity to think.

L'Envoi

Computers have a limited effect
Can recollect—detect—but not reflect.

BIOGRAPHICAL

Admittedly belong to the old school
Won't jog in rubber shoes like one obsessed
But wear bright colored ties, perhaps a vest
Will don blue tam, trimmed plaid, young folks call "cool"

No jeans, or sweat-shirts screaming "where it's at"
Rock-music, blasting waves, leaves me annoyed
Along with sugar, salt, I will avoid
Cholesterol and saturated fat

Scant crescent hair, white as mid-winter snows
Though hearing's less acute I have been told
While cheeks have furrows like a farmer's field
Too often after lunch, I guess I doze
Then drive my car that's more than six years old
Deficiencies ostensibly concealed.

L'Envoi

A fuddy-duddy, old romanticist
Won't shake old habits now—but will persist.

MUSINGS

How wonderful to feel alive again
To romp about in rompers like a child
In innocence so readily beguiled
To roll a hoop, or fly a kite, and then

To turn to indoor games til darkness, when
In weariness I'm comfortably piled
Into my bed to dream of something wild
That's crouching or that's snarling in its den

But when I wake from dreams where I behold
A later world of manifold events
Of loneliness and pain—when I'm bereft
It then occurs to me I'm growing old
No point in litanies of my laments
I speculate about the time that's left.

L'Envoi

But as I contemplate the way I live
It far surpasses the alternative.

THREE THINGS REMAIN

What shall I do with all my life that's left
Take care of me and mine—though they be rental
When they are gone, I'm utterly bereft
This should be obvious—as fundamental

How, meanwhile, shall I use what's mine alone
What am I if I'm lacking thoughts and deeds
What use is there for body, brain, and bone
If no one comes to me for what he needs

When shall I do what everyone must do
I stir my thoughts—I wrinkle up my brow
The answer of the ancient sage is true
There never was a better time than now
Wherefore I study, learn—and with a will
Exert more effort, adding knowledge, skill.

L'Envoi

Though precious gems lie buried in the earth
They can't compare with learning—as to worth.

IN A MELANCHOLY MOOD

Bare trees—their garments tattered—hug the ground
Like saddened, hungry waifs their bodies thinned
Appear to shiver, swaying in the wind
Or whistle softly with a mournful sound

Their only mantle when the cold winds blow
To comfort them against the winter's cold
As slowly or though yearly they grow old
Is covering beneath a shawl of snow

The scene is sad and bleak, and asks for only
The warmth of someone's hand or arm to touch
A wistful hope my friend—if you would call
Remember that it's desolate and lonely
You're in my heart—I love you very much
But coming here would be the best of all.

L'Envoi

Send photo, write a card, or pen a letter
Although embracing you would be much better.

MEDITATION

As creatures age and die, my life keeps growing
Though wars or new disasters pose a strain
While new events occur, I don't complain
But memories of late are overflowing

My hair begins to thin, then grey starts showing
Varieties of thoughts rise in my brain
Though joys are punctured by a random pain
Too many decades pass without my knowing

While melodies delight, more learned from books
Or condiments of which I grew most fond
Romantic moments made for love and kissing
But mirrors tell the truth about my looks
I start to meditate and look beyond
While I'm enjoying life—yet something's missing.

L'Envoi

I try redeeming memories from pawn
But many valued gems seem to be gone.

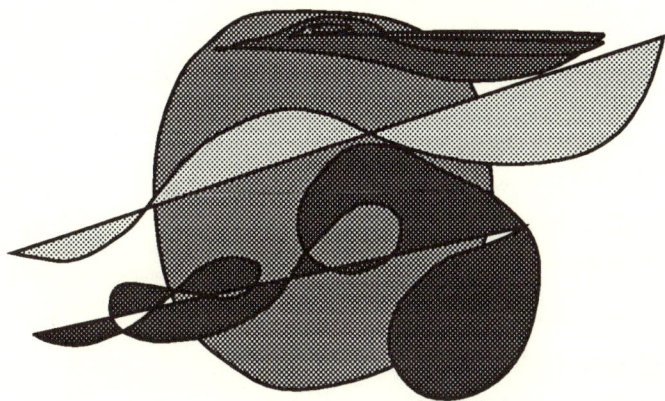

ON POETRY

THE POET'S LAMENT

The poet once was needed to narrate
Events that otherwise were not conveyed
To travel to a distant lord's estate
Recite, and be rewarded for his trade

Now slender rockets flash through distant skies
Fat-bellied airships fly by day and night
Our lightning fax so instantly replies
While television puts us at the site

Since space has shrunk to fractionated size
Transmissions have obliterated time
Perhaps the poet ought to realize
Folks little need his rhythms and his rhyme
What warrants this devotion to the art
Is it the unfelt, or the unborn heart?

L'Envoi

Or justifying art as some surmise
Ratiocinating, or philosophize.

POETICS—AESTHETICS

The hidden joy of poetry I found
In rhythmic rhyming sounds that tempt my ear
Evoking images I see or hear
With tempos slow or swift to soothe or pound

Events or else ideas curl around
Where recollections randomly appear
Of scenic visions—feelings—once held dear
As sentimental viewpoints still abound

Such images and rhythms stimulate
What dormant memories lie in my mind
Remembered—though belonging to a time
When I was younger, thereby recreate
A mood I loved and lost, but hope to find
In verse—especially when it's in rhyme.

L'Envoi

Poetic phrases stir old reference
To be recalled with proper deference.

Anent Professor Stephen Owen's review of Yeh's Anthology
in which he writes: "...poetry, if it survives,
is on its way to somewhere unforeseen."

WHITHER MODERN POETRY

Who can predict where poetry is heading
Will it be like the phoenix that may rise
To soar toward heaven searching farthest skies
Or is it moribund in tear-stained bedding

A needle's eye prepared for different threading
For selling garments that milady buys
To wear at funerals when someone dies
Epithalamium without a wedding

Or have we lost that precious thread reserved
For gathering our folds of black or gray
To chant with choirs in polyphonic parts
Since we were shrived of sins though not deserved
Will it be hymn of praise the way we'd pray
As we gazed heavenward with anxious hearts.

L'Envoi

We trifle with those genres now of choice
In disregard of our most cherished voice.

MIXED MEDIA

A poet paints with words, like blue or yellow
When sketching dainty damsels whom he courts
With simile and metaphor, resorts
To picturing his lady as a cello

With curly head, her neck as graceful, slender
Her bosom and her bottom full and round
The shades and tints are reddish, slightly browned
Her name is Laura, model of her gender

Who dallies with her feelings should be gentle
Brave beau who's drawn to her should finger lightly
When playing on her feelings be concerned
Held by his knees, though warmly sentimental
Behaving toward her kindly and politely
The art of courtship practiced til it's learned.

L'Envoi

With words and music whether modern, quaint
A poet chooses subjects he can paint.

ESSENCES AND PRESENCES

This sonnet's like an ordinary pot
For cooking what could yield a redolence
I sniff, as memories delight my sense
Recalling fragrances that I forgot

Sweet savors rise as food for thought grows hot
Creations bubbling in the present tense
Cross-blending, stirring wonder, joy, suspense
Another dash of garlic—maybe not

Repast would follow as conceptions merge
Neurotransmitters flash to make me feel
The joy of such creations as I know
To offering fresh data at the urge
Distinguishing an image from what's real
I draw on culture for the way to go.

L'Envoi

A sonnet isn't blank, or verse that's free
It is a rarer form of poetry.

WHAT IS A POEM?

A poem is a mirror to reflect
A "truth" perceived within the poet's mind
That looking-glass permitting him to find
An essence, or is not what we expect

We thereupon accept, or else reject
Unless perchance we strongly are inclined
To search for what the poet had designed
Or feel some somesthetical effect

But what of underlying quality
Truth is a seed in wind where leaves have flown
What did the poet say—what did he mean
If poet's truth presumes reality
That truth should blossom from the seed he's sown
With his abiding faith in what he's seen.

L'Envoi

If fog beclouds the picture in the mirror
Our introspection often makes it clearer.

VERSE IS NOT POETRY

A poem resonates—to make one feel
While verse is manufactured mentally
With words assembled incidentally
Like argot—with less cultural appeal

Ideas, data, facts are not emotions
Though verse and poetry both use the word
The soul vibrates when human hearts are stirred
Delight, or sadness nuanced—not trite notions

Where metaphors in verse get mixed—like salad
Become contrived—appear pedestrian
As laborers, when listless, see their job
Though verse is free, or blank—as ode or ballad
Pure poetry, in tones orchestrian
Makes music—so the heart begins to throb.

L'Envoi

True poetry is woman's warm embrace
Strong verses stun and hit you in the face.

FULFILLMENT

Consider—from the time that you awake
You own the hours shortly to unfold
To spend—invest—or waste—unless they're doled
Out working on some worthy things you make

Each valued hour—twenty-four each day
Like precious ore that's hidden in the earth
Is yours to utilize for what it's worth
Lest you delay or look another way

If you but concentrate upon your goal
Use every priceless moment to achieve
What you've been given absolutely free
What parts are missing soon will form a whole
A legacy from Adam and his Eve
Prosaic thoughts evolve as poetry.

L'Envoi

Give all you've got, for while you're giving it
Prose turns to poetry—you're living it.

LINGERING LAMENT

New poets' minds and modes, and moods of feeling
Have wrenched the sweet affections of my heart
As they disdain those rhythmic rhymes once part
Of youthful promise—hurt, that's slow in healing

Indifferences—to which they've grown enamored
Like buildings which expose their inner parts
Unbuttoned way in which they practice arts
Like nails that bend when they are badly hammered

Their willfulness survives—which means they've won
My words and phrases dangle in despair
Their verse and mine seem contradictory
My metered march of sonnets now undone
With their "free verse" in vogue—as I seem "square"
But—have they won a Pyrrhic victory?

L'Envoi

No dactyls, trochees, anapests this time
Five feet of iambs—fourteen lines of rhyme.

PROLIXITY

Away with poets who are esoteric
Whose convoluted moods and metaphors
Bewilder us until the image bores
Suffusing us in vapors atmospheric

With recondite or classical allusions
Surpassing our more modest comprehension
With arcane references of their invention
Inscrutable increases our confusions

Who lead us through remote associations
They've garnered from too much of written lore
Ratioscinating, adding useless stress
Producing, not creating with conflations
As they expound, exuberate, explore
Lack probity and grace that's effortless.

L'Envoi

Those poets often cause us much distress
They seldom write "in phrases effortless."

WHO HAS THE ANSWER?

Why were we born—what purpose ought we serve
For father, mother, siblings, spouse, or nation
A cause for critics, conflict, consternation
Inclining us at times to dodge or swerve

We lurch along in doubt, confused, careening
Through politics, religion, economics
With shattered images or garbled phonics
Endeavoring to find life's real meaning

Try arrogance, or else propriety
As we confront the world of women—men
When dealing with our neighbors, teachers, bosses
In ethnics, culture, or society
As individual or citizen
We live—in hope our wins exceed our losses.

L'Envoi

We query, ponder, gamble til we die
Who, but a poet, ventures a reply.

IMMORTALITY

A famed biologist has now opined
To counter dreads that haunt my daily fears
I should survive one hundred fifteen years
For normal life—from data he could find

With word and image and by artifact
I now can plan a lifetime of such length
Preserving both activities and strength
Though in the end I die—were he exact

But metaphors I leave for generations
So those unborn may one day come to read
What thoughts I had—to tell them of my creed
My faith and love, including consternations
I shall be gone—but if they read my word
My voice, that distant day, may yet be heard.

L'Envoi

While my life passes, time alone can say
Though evanescent—how I feel today.

FOLIO

When first you look into this book of verse
You've turned the knob to enter through a door
Step on the bright red carpet in my store
We may find this occasion to converse

The stanzas speak of science—economics
Perusing people's projects, pleasures, pain
With culture—sociology—the brain
In sonnet form, to cultivate mnemonics

Remembered thoughts like iridescent bubbles
May rise to float around us through the air
Whatever strikes your fancy we can share
In hopes it may distract your mind from troubles
Whatever thoughts of value I have learned
Are offered you with every page that's turned.

L'Envoi

A sonnet may sound silly or seem sage
Be hopeful as you turn another page.

ONE MORE VERSE

If God should whisper in my ear that I
Had time for only one more verse before
My time had come to exit by the door
That everyone goes through when each must die

I'd be hard put, on looking at the sky
When my last day arrives—resist no more
But undertake performance of my chore
To find the words, as time goes flying by

I'd race through philosophic disputations
My deep emotions versus matters mental
Spiritualities or mortal fear
Irreverences, sinful situations
Consider hopefully the transcendental
In great anxiety as death was near.

L'Envoi

In somber mood, I'd brood and then conclude
My sonnet as a sign of rectitude.

GREAT POETS

Great poets are distinguished from dull hacks
By blending intellect with warm affection
Wide learning filtered through deep introspection
Whence world and self are seen through parallax

For parallax permits both eyes to see
Not parallel—whence all that's seen is flat
But eyes which see from angles, since from that
Perception takes on depth effectively

When seen in depth each subject takes on meaning
Whereby an eager reader soon discovers
What feels, reveals, appeals to prior thought
While subjects may be noble, or demeaning
Because events go either way with lovers
The poet finds reward in what he sought.

L'Envoi

The mood you're in may stimulate your mind
Create a verse yourself, if you're inclined.

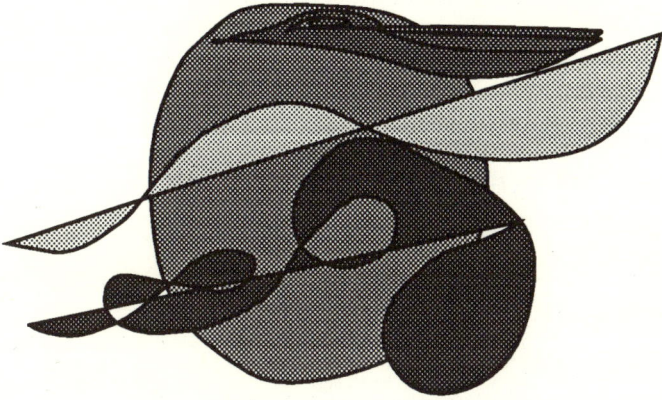

HISTORY

BREAKFAST WITH MALTHUS

I breakfasted with Malthus yesterday
When population came up as a topic
His concepts did not seem too philanthropic
That grim misanthropist had this to say

The demographics must be more systemic
Too many creatures occupy this Earth
Though starving, more insist on giving birth
We need more wars and illness that's endemic

We must reduce the overwhelming census
Get rid of anybody that we can
He stared me in the eye—but sounded sane
I wondered whom he'd chosen to dispense us
To liquidate the child, the woman—man
I asked him who should finally remain.

L'Envoi

He meditated briefly, then he stated
Why all—save us—could be eradicated.

INVOLUTION

How vital is the moisture in the air
To fall as gentle rain on Earth below
Or drifting down in frozen flakes of snow
An omnipresent substance we're aware

Like thought evolving warmly when we care
About the people we have come to know
Or chilled when fellow-man becomes a foe
Phenomena both men and women share

As rain can change from benefit to flood
Destructive when it turns into a torrent
Until the storm wears out as time goes by
So thoughts can turn to war, to drench with blood
With artifacts especially abhorrent
As innocents inevitably die.

L'Envoi

When kindly thought begin to turn amiss
Too often horror follows prejudice.

GROWING UP

We grew like others who attended school
Observing both ridiculous—sublime
But danger lurked—none rose to ridicule
A tyrant who grew crazier with time

A monster snarling hate: a cruel theme
Whose barking voice proclaimed a holy mission
Planned conquering the world—nightmarish dream
But cowed a brilliant nation to submission

Destroyed six million Jews, and many more
With gas and fire—dismissed it with a shrug
Because they were not Aryan to the core
But died a coward—in a hole he dug
He prattled doctrines of inanity
Caused misery with his insanity.

L'Envoi

Incredible the cost, how much was lost
Through Hitler's mad Third Reich—The Holocaust.

BACK TO BASICS

Concerned about big problems in our nation
Aware that something wrong must be afoot
We turn to history to find the root
Our country started out as "Federation"

Revolt from Britain was a war we won
To misconstrue it is irrational
As different states we were not national
Though we're alike, it does not make us one

Let us take back our States—as well we could
Despite the nationalists' forbidding frowns
Regain our cities, villages, and towns
To speak our minds—each in his neighborhood
Ask every patriot to hold the fort
We have an ally in our highest Court.

L'Envoi

The choking grip of nation, were it loosed
Despair and debt might thereby be reduced

BIAS

However man evolved from his creation
His mind informed by circumstance at least
Should keep him from responding like a beast
And treating slights as lethal provocation

Disdain too often comes from prejudice
Permitting action ruthlessly to function
Where harm proceeds indifferent to compunction
To cast enlightenment into abyss

The prophet pleads for man to mend his ways
Whence justice-tempered mercy may evolve
For scabbard swords help woes in time to cease
Then might begin anew man's happy days
When prejudice like poison would dissolve
So mankind might enjoy its days of peace.

L'Envoi

This message it is hoped will not be missed
Its aim—to stay the reckless terrorist.

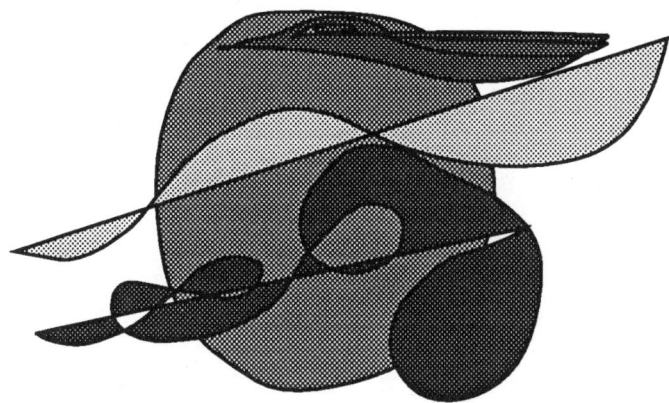

ACCEPTANCE

DON'T JUST SIT THERE

Come take my hand—together we can see
The wondrous treasures of the Universe
Earth—held in place by Sun—for you and me
A radiance by which we can converse

Observe the greens from warming sun and rain
Bright fleecy clouds that texture parts of sky
The very air we breathe—do not disdain
For lack of air all living things will die

Those people who inhabit sea and land
Who want to know of different folks like us
Would like to visit here and understand
The subjects you and I might now discuss
Let's talk of life—and love—and all things good
And hope, when we are through—we're understood.

L'Envoi

Why don't we try to spread the word abroad
Those taking things for granted might be awed.

HELLO

I write for you while dressed in coat and tie
The way I'd come to meet a valued friend
In hopeful mood and manner I extend
My hand to shake your hand—look eye to eye

Aboard our planet, sailing 'neath our sky
On waves of sound and sight we both depend
From our beginnings to some unknown end
We both know when and where, but don't know why

Yet we have much in common even though
Those places where we dwell seem far apart
We both, with hope, pursue a worthwhile goal
Give ear to pundits who pretend to know
Look forward daily with courageous heart
In search of sentiments to stir the soul.

L'Envoi

Despite our prejudice, beliefs, taboos
We're shipmates on this memorable cruise.

VARIATIONS ON A THEME

So many shapes of nature overwhelm
As leaves of trees afar all look alike
Examined closely—round—or like a spike
Catalpa, birch or maple, oak or elm

Or fish—who swim in lakes or in a pool
Though different—caught inside a dipping net
What looked like carp or pike while dripping wet
May bear a close resemblance in a school

When you consider animals as well
Like monkeys, apes, or maybe chimpanzees
They all have heads and arms, are dressed in fur
And if you dwell upon them for a spell
They all have fingers, toes—bend at the knees
Though sometimes hard to tell—'twixt him and her.

L'Envoi

Like people—though we come from different nations
Are much alike—with trifling variations.

ON KNOWLEDGE

We speak of music, writing, and of art
Psychology and sociology
As well as economics and the mart
Or agribusiness, anthropology

With chemistry and physics and the search
For theorems, the mathematical
Come studies past the counting for research
For data deemed as problematical

But when our studied disciplines conclude
Those areas we've chosen to explore
When drinking deep, not merely sip the cup
Examined in assumptive interlude
Our minds (not brains) insist we study more
The learning curve's a spiral going up.

L'Envoi

What goes around may come around, it's true
Goes up for me—is it the same for you?

ON WORSHIP

So much found in the world remains obscure
Some thought the sun arose—we know it doesn't
The cloud at dawn was painted red—it wasn't
Assumed (invalidly) the air was pure

Some thought the Earth was bigger than the sun
Concluded stars they saw would never change
Assumed with daylight stars went out of range
Or midnight came the same for everyone

How color's in the object that one sees
Though rock makes sand which aggregates as stone
Which words they learned to use were always known
Thought God had time to bless them when they'd sneeze
Deemed only they knew how to worship God
How far have they advanced above the clod?

L'Envoi

Insisting on assumptions kept intact
Inhibits one from searching for the fact.

MOODS

My disposition seems to alternate
From feeling high, sloping to one depressed
Because of wicked talk someone expressed
Which caused my airy feelings to deflate

Disconsolate upon this saddened state
Like charged with guilt—remaining unconfessed
I sulk and grouse like someone dispossessed
As though I were an evil reprobate

In time my over-burdened heart will lighten
As any malady will run its course
I'm shrived of sin and guilt—there was no crime
No ugly hate or threat remains to frighten
The therapy evolving from the source
Confessor, mentor, savior—Father Time.

L'Envoi

If some day you should feel let down and blue
Stand firm, my friend, for time will rescue you.

IMPROVING THIS WORLD

What troubles me is not a mystery
When I am introspective or concerned
About this world—but those who have not learned
My novel way of viewing history

Will find this world a harried place to be
Depending on the problems once discerned
It's not the restful place for which we've yearned
But if you wonder what on Earth I see

No changes in quotidian routine
Of family, or city, state or nation
But change myself is all that I can do
I simply interpose myself between
All else and me—using imagination
To build a better scene for me to view.

L'Envoi

Our universe improves as I perceive it
While I keep trying harder—and believe it.

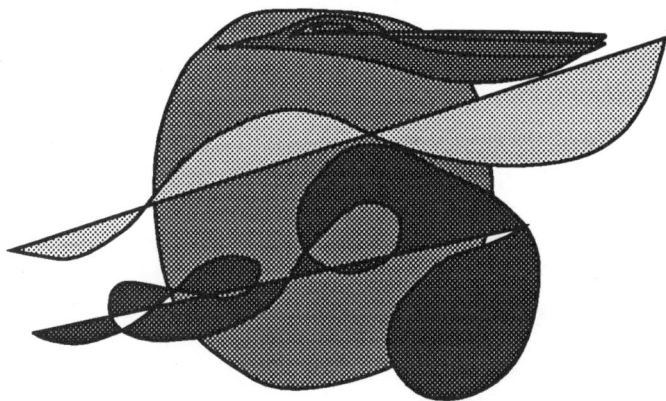

COMMENTARY

INSPIRATION

When trivia with meaningless combine
To spade the earth where my remains will lie
While I pretend to live—instead I die
Unripened fruit to wither on the vine

This knob-like brain which rests upon my spine
Might flourish and be fruitful if I try
But I must first bestir myself to ply
With will to change my spiritless design

I must begin to energize the arc
Which flashes—whence I suddenly advert
To join the old with new so I detect
Awareness of the coming of a spark
To leap between two images inert
Reposing fallow in my intellect.

L'Envoi

However dull and pointless life may seem
Fulfillment may lie hidden in a dream.

ON FIRST LOOKING INTO RILKE'S SONNETS TO ORPHEUS

When first you saw the light of day my friend
Your mother held you in her womb no longer
Thenceforward you held her as you grew stronger
Thus circumscribing life until its end

For mother, who was someone you could hold
Intimately, always your possession
Diurnally, pursuing your progression
From tender youth, until you both grew old

All you've acquired—held by you in fee
With titles and certificates you show
Regardless of how many, or how few
The day will come when you can clearly see
How truth evolves—whereby you rightly know
Whatever you may hold—is holding you.

L'Envoi

If you discover you've become possessive
Change your perspective, lest you grow obsessive.

UNIQUE

Miraculous—how we were all begun
From all religions, kingdoms, countries, nations
How insignificant in calculations
Of several billion people—each is one

What does it mean to be among the number
Who rise each day to look for drink and food
To study, work, or play—or sit and brood
As each maneuvers, then returns to slumber

Inscrutable, the mystery of each
Why were we born—to whom do we belong
Who owes us aught—what ends should each one seek
We question, wonder, pray, explore, beseech
How was our milieu formed with "right" and "wrong"
How did each happen to be here—unique?

L'Envoi

No certainty—all things are mutable
Enjoy this world, although inscrutable.

WHEN THIS CIVILIZATION IS GONE

In forest glen or maybe cities massed
Long after we are gone, but others live
Sophisticated or then primitive
When ten-or-twenty-thousand years have passed

Technologies, like magic—though achieved
Admittedly unprecedented boon
Our generation walking on the moon
Though no one in the past would have believed

Our species gone—a different-looking creature
Observes a vehicle he cannot start
Our televisions and computers dark
Then mystified—will seek a future teacher
Though they remain a small or greater part
What have we gained, thus having made our mark?

L'Envoi

Civilizations rise, then disappear
Each will encounter love, and greed, and fear.

A FRIEND

Will share with you a sudden risk of harm
When fortune might have smiled, but turns its back
As threat arises—poised for its attack
A friend will offer ear and readied arm

Whose counsel steadies you in your distress
Reviews your options, strategies, and choice
Is at your side with reassuring voice
As hurtful circumstance begins to press

Will strengthen you when your resolve is weak
Reminds you that a threat might be deceptive
But if the harm should strike will share your sorrow
When life is at its worst and all looks bleak
Enables you to see life in perspective
For yesterday, today, and for tomorrow.

L'Envoi

They're hard to find—you're lucky when you see one
What's more—to have a friend, you've got to be one.

WHAT TIME IS IT?

What is the time, you ask—I'll tell you now
It's half past time you should pick up the phone
To call somebody sitting all alone
Whose circumstances little will allow

It's also well past time you sat and wrote
To someone watching through the window pane
Who sees too little sunshine, too much rain
Who would be very pleased to get your note

It's also getting late you realize
The time no longer tarries—it has fled
Because you were too seldom in the mood
To lift your downcast eyes and search the skies
But now before too late, when you are dead
Thank God for whom you are—in gratitude.

L'Envoi

The gifts of sight, of memory, of speech
Enjoy them now, before they're out of reach.

GENERATIONAL

In every generation life will change
As youngsters versus elders start to duel
The elders kind, with youngsters often cruel
As neither seems inclined toward fair exchange

Though values in the different groups may vary
When elders grouch about how young behave
As elders cling to customs they would save
While young imprudently do not seem wary

It's sad to find the scenes erupt in quarrels
When voices rise to higher decibels
As angers rise in everybody's heart
The issue often has to do with morals
As youngsters deem their newer view excels
How reconcile them both before they part?

L'Envoi

The elders who compel the child's conformance
May wind up with the opposite performance.

NEW FAMILIES

Should we be troubled by anomalies
Which economics made eventual
Resigned to what is now conventional
Irregularities among our families

In genders, patterns currently so varied
With numbers, kinds, durations, and degrees
Composed of he's and he's, and she's and she's
And even he's and she's who stay unmarried

No longer comic, quaint, or humorous
Inane or stupid, in our current views
Impetuousness or rascality
With AIDS, betrayal, crimes so numerous
Is now the time to reinstate taboos
With morals lost in informality.

L'Envoi

Eradicate the rancor, blunt the blame
Revive some old taboos—like sense of shame.

ON LOOKING FORWARD

When I, in optimism, baited fate
Let hope arise, til reaching expectation
Allowed myself presumptions of elation
To favor me at some upcoming date

I squiggle with delight as I await
Exciting moments in anticipation
A sense of triumph at this elevation
An undeniably delicious state

Event at last arrives—when time's gone by
My heart beats quicker as the climax nears
With destiny on time for its appointment
That instant, in the flutter of an eye
My hopes reversed—from cheers, to fears—or tears
To overwhelming mood of disappointment.

L'Envoi

I'll be more diligent when next I care
For hope is vain—unless I first prepare.

ON GETTING AGGRAVATED

When, in the course of study, work, or play
An irritating person makes you halt
Consider first—are you the one at fault
If so, then you should change without delay

But if you're in the right, don't waste your day
With one whose brains are buried in a vault
With anyone who isn't worth his salt
But hope the mope will shortly go away

To be upset is foolish, gains you little
You harm yourself when your emotions hurt
You lose—no matter how much it's debated
You're wise to treat it like a bit of spittle
Then terminate it—gracefully—or curt
But let the thoughtless one get aggravated.

L'Envoi

Don't waste your time in generous forgiving
Move on to happy, more rewarding living.

HISTORY LESSON

When young—while hearing's sharp, eyes not yet dim
No missing teeth to bite and grind your food
Your parts all work—taste, smell, and strength are good
Those hips and bellies still are firm and slim

Your eagerness in jumping to conclusions
Is instantaneous upon occasion
In personal, or social situation
As faith creates unlimited illusions

But as your body, then your mind, matures
Through passing decades, do not be afraid
On loss, there's gain, as you become more sage
With new experience becoming yours
When spirits—high or low—cannot be stayed
But hesitate before you turn this page.

L'Envoi

Each moment blends both truth and mystery
This moment gone, becomes your history.

IN CASE OF IRE—WALK

If death is irreversible—so be it
I'll make the best of what I have in hand
What's best among the objects that I've scanned
The highest goal to reach for as I see it

From slavish habits—first—I'd better free it
From paths of least resistance—make a stand
Bad habits are our masters, left unplanned
Get in the game instead of referee it

Our ways grow into habits as we go
The good—the bad—though some are in between
Some leave us sad, or fill us with elation
The best advice to offer that I know
Distinguish 'twixt the messy and the clean
And draw deep breaths—for better inspiration.

L'Envoi

Frustrated? Find it difficult to smile?
Then try my way and walk another mile.

ON DUTY

Be for yourself—a fundamental must
But for yourself alone will come to naught
Unless you help another and have taught
What thoughts and acts are fair—what deeds are just

You should be worthy of another's trust
These are the attributes that should be sought
To cultivate a life that isn't fraught
With discontent, despair, or worse—disgust

There should be time for study, work, and rest
Sweet hours planned for sheer, light-hearted play
For tales of heroes—verses 'neath the bough
As peaceful moments alternate with zest
Provide for meditation every day
Make this a ritual—and start it now.

L'Envoi

Who fills a life with deeds of noble duty
May find that life achieving boundless beauty.

HUMANITIES

There is a time for peace when folks enjoy
A chance for labor, study, shop, or clerk
Produce—exhibit their creative work
Fulfill themselves—employ but not destroy

There is a time for talk—discuss intently
Probe thoughts dissolving arrant prejudice
Reviewing passions when some act amiss
With words not hammered in but tendered gently

There is a time when troubled to the core
We take up arms, when reasoning has ended
When truth and justice need to be defended
When there seems no alternative save war
But when that time has passed, no further fighting
There's time for music, painting, and for writing.

L'Envoi

Of all we undertake and hope to please
Rewards await us in humanities.

IN SUM

I think—therefore I hope to comprehend
The nature of the world, including man
Conceive a starting point—where life began
Aware that what begins must likewise end

As thoughts, ideas, words begin to lend
A sense of form and function for my plan
Then, with the eye that's in my mind, I scan
What others miss, but I can apprehend

I shall survive the years my heart will beat
As culture brings about its change in fashions
Distinguishing fictitious from the real
Yet measuring all life in pounds or feet
While I restrained the gamut of my passions
I may have missed the gist of what I feel.

L'Envoi

Events, with ideologies and notions
Dissolve—what's left is finally emotions.

74

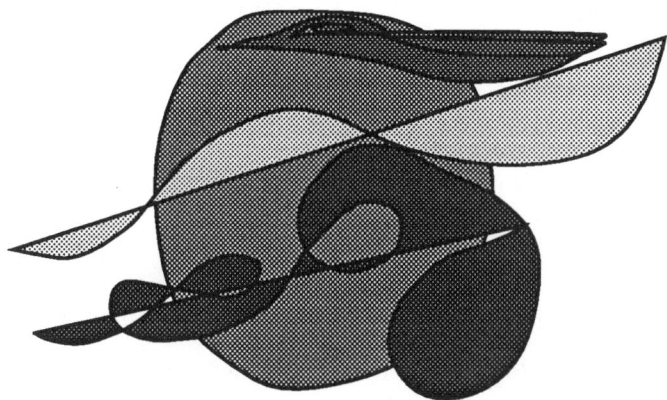

VIEWPOINTS

TO THE NEXT CENTURY

Please board my bus—together we can ride
Into the century that beckons us
Review anew, deliberate, discuss
Why twenty and the twenty-first divide

Why do we measure articles, or years
How does the day that's after or before
Leave us with something less, or give us more
Evoking sadness, or the cup that cheers

We viewed our planet Earth, then traveled higher
To search for life or humans out in space
If, with advanced technology, we prod
We might find something wonderful, or dire
Depending on what's in the other place
Unless, of course, we can discover God.

L'Envoi

By measuring, we quantify—we know
So get on board to change the status quo.

WHAT IS LIFE?

Arriving from an unexpected birth
Each child unique—a daughter or a son
What can we do when all is said and done
While we are here, exploring planet Earth

Our years will be diffused with tears and mirth
With playing games indoors or in the sun
Recalling times we lost—the few we won
Or economics, get our money's worth

It could be business—sales, accounting, clerks
Time spent inside a factory or mill
Or teaching what some other teachers taught
There's challenge in these different kinds of works
If each is so disposed, or has the will
For life is shaped by goals each one has sought.

L'Envoi

But every one—when all is said and done
Always depends upon some other one.

WHAT'S A THING?

A "thing" can be a little piece of string
From Maupassant—became a famous tale
To sailors it may be a worn-out sail
A feather fallen from a swallow's wing

It also may describe a bit of lint
A baby's yellow plastic truck that's broken
A talisman that's undefined, a token
Or pebble in a boot that hurts like flint

A "thing" can look familiar, or be odd
It might be either noisy or quiescent
A Christian's cross, or Muslim's star and crescent
A "thing" can be a stick with which to prod
A shard may seem to be a "thing" for scholars
From ancient tombs—it could be worth big dollars.

L'Envoi

The value of an object old or new
Depends on what the thing is worth to you.

WHAT'S ANYTHING WORTH?

Consider what we humans note on Earth
A man or beast, or things that are inert
What pleased us, or conversely may have hurt
Three thoughts control—ideals, values, worth

Ideals represent what is admired
While values represent what we prefer
But what we try for—held by him or her
Is "worth"—whatever's ardently desired

What others own or have, that we have not
Provokes our pride, or generates our greed
What currently, consensus calls "pizzazz"
What, in the language of the streets, is "hot"
Although it may not be that which we need
It's what we lack, but what another has.

L'Envoi

Though buried deep, we'd struggle to unearth it
Despite the fact the darn thing isn't worth it.

AMERICA

This land of beauty—happiness and hope
Of wisdom in the way that life is led
Where most religious views are taught (or shed)
Mohammed, Jesus, Moses, and the Pope

Though some impiously may try to cope
With faith in circling zodiacs instead
Despite the incongruities they've read
They cast about to find a horoscope

From sacred Testaments, Old, New, Koran
In mosque and temple, synagogue and church
The Vedas read—or other holy word
Where nature-lovers find their god in Pan
The fundamentalists leave in the lurch
What we find good, but they deem is absurd.

L'Envoi

In this great nation that we hold so dear
The arrogant may sneer—til death is near.

VIEWPOINTS

As you peruse this verse from title down
Indifference—or bated expectation
Depends, of course, on your imagination
You may be bored, or smile, or even frown

Is this reality, or just pretend
As I suggest, infer, imply, allude
Which may communicate my attitude
Assumptive—or it's actual—at end

Our different cultures may distort our logic
Divergent aspects coming into play
As we endeavor both to lay truth bare
Add chemicals affecting biologic
Will different views appear—like night and day
Or are there universals we can share?

L'Envoi

Each brings a story from the past which bears
Upon how much or little each one cares.

HORIZONS

All thought requires limits—we can't see
Can't grasp, nor understand, nor comprehend
Can't visualize an object to its end
When thoughts so wander to infinity

Like any picture which requires a base
Two sides to hold the top and thereby frame
An object or idea—not the same
As others with another's form or case

However great the strides our culture gains
How far we reach until the farthest skies
Or tiny—which we fasten both our eyes on
However brilliant ours or others' brains
There's something past the limits of our eyes
We cannot see beyond our own horizon.

L'Envoi

How far another sees—beyond our own
Is how we go, from unknown to the known.

BOTTLES

A mind is like a bottle or a jar
Though empty, it can readily be filled
Or like a mouth, whence volumes can be spilled
If your imagination runs that far

May be transparent, or its fluids hid
Inside a large container, or a small
It could be cracked, as happens in a fall
Or bought—depending on what someone bid

Both are receptacles—each has its worth
Which might have precious value or be cheap
Diluted, or a vintage proud to store
When brains or artifacts are found on Earth
However tall or small, each lets you keep
The image—simile or metaphor.

L'Envoi

Psychiatrists advise—to hasten healings
Don't try to bottle-up your guilty feelings.

BEAUTY

Perfection—found in scene—or sound or thing
Traditional, new fashioned, or surreal
An image apperceived by which you feel
A pregnant yearning, which fulfilled can bring

Warm recollections of a happening
That earlier had infinite appeal
Remembered tones of distant bells that peal
Or sacred songs familiar choirs sing

Combining cherished past with each new day
Recalling former pleasures, precious things
Sensations which delighted, in review
Of crafted metal—glass—or wood—or clay
From stirring drums and horns, melodic strings
Beauty perceived—becomes a part of you.

L'Envoi

But if you're searching yet, with heart and sinew
Beauty awaits if only you continue.

NO ENCUMBRANCES

No unencumbered self—each one of us
Becomes enslaved by prophet or by faith
Although a prophet may be deemed a wraith
A subject fit to argue and discuss

Who are we, of what matter are we made
Enlightenment as taught in many schools
Can demonstrate we're merely molecules
But in adversity, whence comes our aid

As animals, when chilled, we seek a warming
If hot, we yearn to find a place that's cool
Or thirsty, seek a satisfying drink
Our human lives are process—with performing
We vote (or don't) for candidates to rule
Preoccupied—we feel, but seldom think.

L'Envoi

Our complex human ways impose restraint
Alternatively—animal or saint.

LENDING AN EAR

We have no say about our being born
We can't select our parents, or the site
Or culture—or skin color—dark or light
We're like a kernel on an ear of corn

We like to be like others on the cob
But not exactly, since we're each unique
As we appear, from our genetic streak
On playing field, at school, or on the job

Since sunny summer seasons swiftly yield
Their gentle natures warm and salutary
Corn ripens, then the leaves start turning dry
We, like the corn, take risks out in the field
Because in every lifetime some things vary
But plants and people resolutely try.

L'Envoi

Though each is born from seed it can't select
How fortunate we are in retrospect.

BIO LOGIC

Once, good or evil gods were thought to be
Potential powers, baneful type, or kind
But time has brought us to a different mind
On what we think controls our destiny

When swelling or a redness says we're ill
As bad bacteria so often do it
Today we say, elated, since we knew it
We overcome it with a doctor's pill

Gods, once believed by man, are in decline
A god is neither noble king, nor rogue
No angry devils, new gods glorious
When sickness strikes your family or mine
Mankind adopts whatever is in vogue
Like science—which is now victorious.

L'Envoi

Beware of pills to gain euphoric bliss
They bring depression, death, and the abyss.

BEING MORAL

Moods vary—peace may crumble into quarrel
When fright ensues, impelling flight or fight
Except for what society deems "right"
Decreeing ways we understand as moral

An outside force mandates a person mayn't
React with violence—it offers clues
About the wiser way for us to choose
By using words, which signify restraint

Morality refers to wrong or right
What is permissible and what is not
Providing rules when you are on the scene
You need not flee, nor kick and claw or bite
If either one of you is getting "hot"
Do not rely on enzyme or a gene.

L'Envoi

Morality is better than dissension
Avoiding injury when in contention.

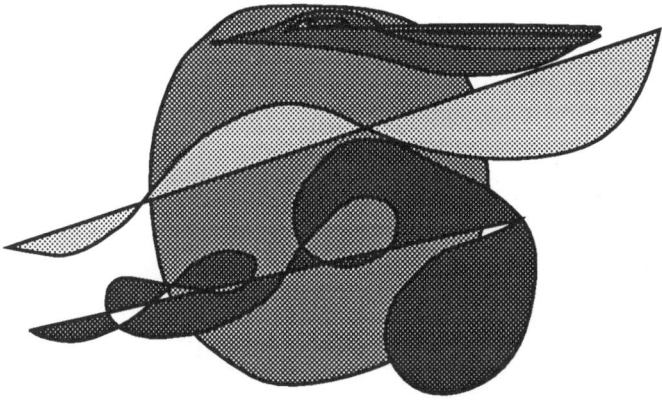

RELIGION

CURRENT TESTAMENT

Electric charges pierce the cloudy air
I trembled when it seemed that He came down
Seemed sad but sympathetic—wore a frown
As wires whispered and the winds declare

With grieving sounds implying His despair
That murmured softly, spreading through the town
Oblivious of skin—white, black, or brown
Or social status—whether clothed or bare

"Your ideologies cause interference
Confusing 'sin' with 'virtue'—right with wrong
Assumptions—doubts—increase in marked degree
Experience and logic lend coherence
Restore morality—where you belong
For certainty, remember, start with 'Me.'"

L'Envoi

Electric sparks subsided—winds were still
My trembling stopped, my echo said, "I will."

EAST OR WEST—WHICH ONE IS BEST?

Throughout the places Western clergy trod
As missionaries in localities
They quote our prophets on moralities
While thumping Bibles—praise the Word of God

Since every vice originates in sin
Which has a way of sticking in our craw
Then hardens into lasting rules of law
Though Satan in the Garden's wearing thin

Still, prophets of the Moslems, Christians, Jews
Engender guilt—we jeopardize our souls
If we should sin, at death, we'll find no peace
I sometimes wonder if we stand to lose
While praying like the Easterners for goals
Like Voodoo, Babist, Hindu, or Chinese.

L'Envoi

But for the nonce—I think I'll pass on this
While I reflect upon my prejudice.

ON FUNDAMENTALISM

You may know all about the birds and bees
Or fertilizing eggs, and flowers, too
But this may be the proper time for you
To ventilate your ideologies

Ideas—like the world at its Creation
Which some demur upon, or introspect
Since questioning of Bibles is suspect
All products of someone's imagination

While "facts" assumed by us may not be real
Our "proof" may be a syllogistic lie
Some "truths" can't be relied on to the letter
We seem to live and die by what we feel
Adopt another's faith, or simply try
Extrapolating into something better.

L'Envoi

Consider Eden, man's depravity
Then reconsider now—with gravity.

BIBLE THUMPING

Only Almighty God could first conceive
A plan to turn a nothingness—no sky
No land or sea or air billowing by
Bleak emptiness that nothing could relieve

Singly, with mighty arm, He could achieve
More stars than we on Earth can quantify
In constellations that no human eye
Could grasp—not even all the heirs of Eve

But are those bibles right which undertake
To place the odium of mortal sin
Upon a woman blatantly maligned
Whose innocence man undertook to make
Consummate guilt, intending to begin
Thereafter, as the master of mankind?

L'Envoi

For only she was perfectly designed
To bear the future heirs of humankind.

ERUDITION

When young, we were persuaded, taught, cajoled
By many who, in greater wisdom, found
In water, air, below or on the ground
Bacteria, genes, enzymes, virus, mold

Once known as ether, vapors at some schools
In upper atmospheres, or caves, or graves
In other places, particles, or waves
But currently described as molecules

How long Creation took, while Someone toyed
With minerals and vegetables, a bird
Insects and animals, plus human creatures
To fill an emptiness, a total void
Can we believe what prophets saw or heard
When every passing day we find new features.

L'Envoi

We shouldn't let such major problems tense us
For "truth," it seems, reposes in consensus.

GILGAMESH

Sumerians came early on the scene
To tell of mortal man and his travails
Gilgamesh Epic helps one early glean
Illumination through their mythic tales

It tells of Enkaidu—half-god half-man
Conversing with wild animals with ease
He sinned—and through a pagan goddess' plan
Lost immortality beneath the seas

The mystery of death beguiles us all
For when we die, our lives seem wisps of smoke
What wisdom we accumulate seems small
Since hearsay underlies the words "God spoke"
What Testaments our different faiths assert
Were meant to help mankind—and not to hurt.

L'Envoi

Religionists should now repudiate
The stupid clergyman who dwells on "hate."

GIVE THANKS

Our daily chores are waiting to be done
We shower, dress, have breakfast—then we drive
But what keeps every one of us alive
To do "our thing"—the same for everyone

The air we breathe—our hearts—the food we eat
A joinder of an ovum with a sperm
Our muscles underneath our epiderm
Enable us to move our hands and feet

We march along in motley serried ranks
With family, or work, with neighbors, friends
The muffled march of millions never ends
Who stops to think of gratitude gives thanks
Do rich and famous—does the lowly clod
For all our gifts do we say thanks to God?

L'Envoi

Though crowded with events throughout the day
Since life is transient, take the time to pray.

SONNET FOR SABBATH

A verse can serve to shut the world out
To hear instead a voice that may be near
Dissolving vague uneasiness, or fear
A Sabbath to relieve the pain of doubt

Relax with feelings out beyond the mind
Or in your mind, but stirring your recall
A past occurrence, not what might befall
But warm sensations you are pleased to find

It raises consciousness from sublimation
Lifts pressures when your heart is overwrought
Distractions you resent, but must condone
Perhaps revives a feeling of elation
With word, or image of a fleeting thought
Of something that uniquely is your own.

L'Envoi

Review what happy thoughts might fill your cup
You could be pleased, my friend, by what comes up.

HEAVENLY DAYS

Almighty God had grossly been offended
Henceforth no others would be resurrected
Elijah, Jesus, Moses were dejected
By endless strife of humans not intended

Redemption would no longer be extended
Not even pious ones whose lives were led
In innocence—they feared a void instead
As dread arose, all dispensation ended

They then turned to Mohammed and decried
The sword of Islam had spilled too much blood
All Christians, Jews, and Muslims must be told
Lay down your arms and peacefully abide
Lest Earth explode or suffer further flood
Like Noah in his Ark in days of old.

L'Envoi

Unless wars end, our Earth with blossoms fair
Could evanesce—dissolve in cosmic air.

BLIND FAITH

Within our hopeful minds we can conceive
Ideas new and old that some suggest
Which add small value to our treasure chest
But we are gullible to still believe

Especially when some claim they receive
Reality—where wise men won't invest
Ideas fraught with guile, which are expressed
By clerics who, self-interested, deceive

With notions claiming dead will be revived
Redeemed from lives the clergymen call sin
Imagined as conceivably achieved
Are rather to be scoffed at—be short lived
As fantasy that only zealots spin
Expecting that our purse will be relieved.

L'Envoi

They trumpet vengeful devils as abroad
Methinks their notions seriously flawed.

DOWNRIGHT DIVINE

The world began when God chose to invent
Three things—a solid, liquid, and a gas
Amazing—this exiguous event
Brought our fantastic universe to pass

Our planet orbiting by gravity
Brought sun, wind, rain, plants, animals galore
Fish swimming waters in concavity
Birds soaring through the air—Earth holds much more

Came man who joined with woman whereby each
Contributing, could breed as they desired
Formed minds and memories, endowed with speech
Each generation similarly sired
Then God smote Mount Moriah with a rift
Gave Moses Ten Commandments—as a gift.

L'Envoi

Civilizations grew apace because
Mankind made artifacts, but lived by laws.

HARMONY

Morality in families preserves
A reverence for God—and deep respect
For human life in each religion, sect
There duty is implanted as each serves

Compassionate Authority observes
Those equal rights each person should expect
To grant and to enjoy—in retrospect
What civilized society conserves

There, orderly behavior will result
From most religions, so that each achieves
Fulfillment of his capabilities
Emerging youth, each sibling and adult
Enjoying harmony as each perceives
His freedom and response-abilities.

L'Envoi

Depart from where the Sunnis-Shiites dwell
For their Koran makes you an infidel.

ASSUMPTIONS

Believers versus non-believers vie
About the world's Creation and its cause
Both recognize perfection—see its flaws
That gives us life, although we all must die

Religious ideologists may try
To legislate—proposing diverse laws
Which make opponents furious because
Their "facts" may be assumptive, or a lie

Their "facts" from testimonials arise
From votaries with passionate concern
Proclaiming "truth" that warrants their reliance
But time reduces miracles to size
Perceptive students ultimately learn
Assumptions underlie prayer and science.

L'Envoi

While various assumptions linger long
They serve—til something better comes along.

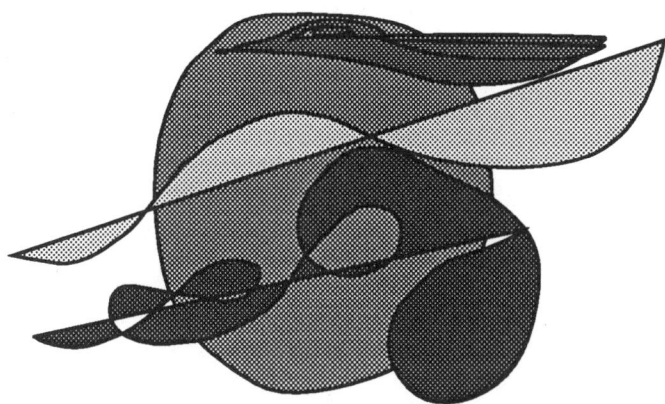

SCIENCE AND TECHNOLOGY

ENVIRONMENTALIST

Sperm enters ovum—changes then begin
Continue through the sound of birthing cries
The infant grows, along with next of kin
Inexorable—til the human dies

While humans impact the environment
Environment impacts on them as well
Sometimes according to what humans meant
Or uncontrolled, in places where they dwell

We try, and thus involve variety
Informed by ambiance of different kind
Religious, ethnic, each society
Though biologic—grows as well in mind
Transformed by growth, since culture's changing, too
Alike with nature—old gets mixed with new.

L'Envoi

Clean water, air and earth, and lack of strife
Grant us and progeny a longer life.

QUESTION

As restful night dissolves each day's concerns
A precious day will dawn with every season
In steady rhythm, lacking rhyme or reason
Earth soundlessly continuing its turns

As mountains silently wear down their mass
Or insects sting, birds swoop upon their wings
While verses cannot change like growing things
They may become like shards of shattered glass

Broad oceans filled with fish and giant mammals
High tides responding to the sun and moon
White fleecy clouds that wander through the sky
A torrid desert with its fleets of camels
The taste of luscious fruit, a simple tune
But no one in the world to tell us why.

L'Envoi

Or lightning, that precedes and causes thunder
As air explodes—another cause for wonder.

APPERCEPTION

'Twixt scientist and poet—stretches space
Which varies from the narrow to the vast
As each gains insights from a different base
Yet both find "truth" revealed—like metal cast

A scientist informs the intellect
With concepts culled from careful calculations
Perceptively examined, which detect
Some hitherto unfathomed correlations

While poets ponder painfully each passion
Then voice with eloquence, in rhythmic art
Their sensitive response to hurt—compassion
That resonates vibrations of the heart
We study both, we yearn to grasp the gist
And ponder—as we wander—in the mist.

L'Envoi

The scientist must change—as time reveals
More constant is the way the poet feels.

MOISTURE

The rains that rattled window panes to settle
In rivulets that ran into the ground
Became the hydrostatics rootlets found
While morning dew was glinting on the petal

When steam came screaming from the boiling kettle
Or thunder from the clouds began to sound
And signal stormy rains would soon abound
To penetrate with rust through sheets of metal

Our noses drip from tears that wash the eye
As sweat evaporates we soon feel cool
Or we encounter thirst, then seek a drink
We loll our tongues about if we seem dry
When we grow old we often start to drool
In fact this print needs liquid in the ink.

L'Envoi

From sky to stream, lake, river out to sea
With water lacking, where would mankind be?

EARLY MORNING FLIGHT

When unexpectedly I heard a beep
Inside my head, of new realities
Involving possible legalities
My fantasies prepared to make a leap

What if—my mental process starts to tinker
As I proceed to reconstruct a part
Invented recently—state of the art
While light emerges as a flashing blinker

By redesigning ratchet notches or
Constructing different orbits which could flip
A switch, thereby perform another task
The world would beat a pathway to my door
Though it requires a different microchip
If only I knew somebody to ask.

L'Envoi

I thought of millions it would quickly make me
Just then, my clock-alarm began to wake me.

108

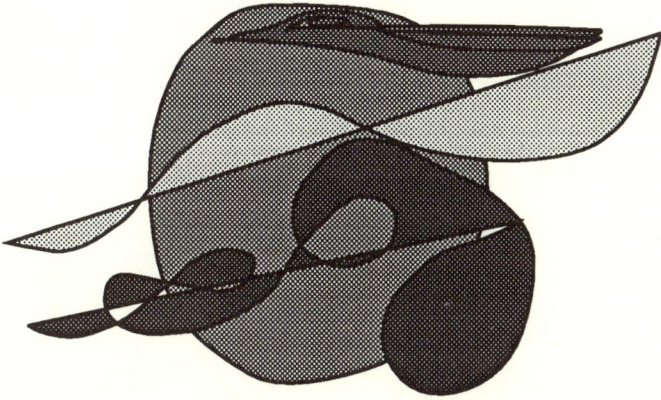

THANKS

HYMN OF GRATITUDE

Thank you sweet Earth for taking us on board
We promise to be faithful to your needs
Protect your air and water, land and seeds
Conserve what oil and gas you wisely stored

Draw warmth from red and gold found in the sun
A charming range of color in the light
Green grass, blue sky, with puffy clouds of white
The quiet black of night when day is done

What roots we find maturing in the earth
Rich ripened fruit that grows upon the vine
Sharp flavor of the salt that's in the brine
We value and appreciate their worth
However this great planet first began
For ever-loving woman, fellow man.

L'Envoi

Through hurried, harried, heedless nights and days
We stop to render words of loving praise.

IN THE BEGINNING

Before creation—nothing—entropy
A seamless, windless space sans sea or ground
No sweet nor noxious smells, stillness profound
Nor sight—black void enduring endlessly

With neither sky nor cloud—infinity
Cold, desolate, the world unformed, unbound
Not even particle or wave was found
All meaningless, without reality

An essence grew more densely in the dark
K-mesons streaking farther into night
Then matter, anti-matter—worlds to be
Imploded, came the star, with gluon, quark
As universes changed from dark to light
Fortuitous—or else divinity.

L'Envoi

What of the future, who can wisely say
We're born—we live—be thankful every day.

HOLIDAY

Whom shall I thank when days are bright and sunny
Depressing problems suddenly dissolved
The pinch of inconveniences resolved
Concerned with neither power, jewels, nor money

A broad-arched sky, landscape around me spacious
A quiet time—no omnipresent speech
Familiar pleasant sounds within my reach
My privacy preferred to the loquacious

Insides unfold—with sense of obligation
Where independence jostling with transcendence
Begins to penetrate this pleasant mood
That deepens and enlarges my sensation
As duty grows, so too, does my dependence
How shall I best express my gratitude?

L'Envoi

I thank this chance to wrinkle up my brow
With gratitude at being here, and now.

MANY THANKS

Dear World—when almost all is said and done
With endless planets floating everywhere
Our shining seas, rich land and vibrant air
This Earth of ours beyond comparison

We tenants, who explore your lovely sphere
Beyond our houses, gardens, flowers, fences
Enjoying all our five and other senses
Inform you that to us, you're very dear

Beginning from the moment each arrives
Continuing through childhood, youth, and age
For all the joys it's possible to know
We thank you for the gifts of all our lives
Tomorrow's promise, plus our heritage
With heart-felt gratitude we seldom show.

L'Envoi

We cherish you, reject the spurious
But keep on searching since we're curious.

CONTEST

While real or romantic, marks dissension
We feel—which then results in consequence
Since differences between them are immense
Producing moods we recognize, as tension

When passion rises, generating heat
Excitement makes vibrations that we feel
Is this imagination—is it real
Should we use head, or heart, or maybe feet

If "consequence" is subject to prediction
Communicating words, or sometimes germs
Health hazards—HIV that's positive
Our see-saw pivots firmly on conviction
Since each of us must someday comes to terms
Deciding on which way we want to live.

L'Envoi

While music, writing, art enrich our days
Each situation calls for yeas, or nays.

LAST WORDS

Since life can end as quickly as a wink
Whence suddenly I may no longer be
No oxygen, or some catastrophe
What is the greatest thought that I can think

Of all the bright ideas, times, events
Experiences, inadvertencies
Religious urges, or philosophies
What final words—what rare or common sense

My youth was often filled with times of yearning
To win a game where I became the star
Loving society, and solitude
Enriching were the times I spent in learning
As thinking yields—emotions rise—by far
My deepest feeling, one of gratitude.

L'Envoi

Life grants its own rewards, that notion ranks
Highest of all—which generates my thanks.

TIME FLIES

I sense time passing, yet I always know
How cherished are the moments flying by
Whether I skip or stroll, sit, stand or lie
An oxymoron, since it's status quo

Whatever tensions I may undergo
However much I sing, inveigh, or cry
How frank and earnest, shy or sly am I
With clenched fist beating on my breast to show

Whether I see epiphanies, or sprites
Or images my fingers cannot touch
Which stand transfixed, or wander by the way
What congregation—blacks, or browns, or whites
With all their prayers, though they try as much
Can bring back vestiges of yesterday?

L'Envoi

I have no fear, regret, nor hint of sorrow
I know I can do better on the morrow.

SPECULATION

The way to please ourselves, both you and I
Survey the list of possibilities
Then seize the moment, falling on our knees
In gratitude for life, before we die

Lie on a grassy sward—gaze at the sky
Historic home of all divinities
Stroll in serenity through leafy trees
Or read a tale so sad it makes us cry

Assuming we have normal attributes
Our learning and our skills somewhat near par
Our usual reaction's not too odd
Gone are our youthful joys of loud disputes
Religion waning toward the secular
Imagine what goes through the mind of God.

L'Envoi

With mankind in His image, to the letter
Good God—how could we function here much better.

DURABLE ORNAMENT

Our Jeweled Universe: Sun, Space, and Earth
A diamond timepiece chronicling life's flow
Red Dawn, gold rays, blue sky, the moon's orange glow
Sun glints at poles, blazes Equator's girth

Black satin nights with galaxies no dearth
Of silver stars set brilliantly to show
In solar-lunar harmony, that though
We strut bejeweled, a doubt still haunts our birth

Computers flash with flick of access key
Atomic miracles we cherish/mourn
Astounding Age, unlimited in scope
Except no calculus for certainty
Which leaves as legacy for those unborn
Three tarnished trinkets—Beauty, Wisdom, Hope.

L'Envoi

As beauty sullies first, blindly we grope
Our wisdom though uncertain, still we hope.